The poems in this anthology are the winning entries in the 2009 FLOW for All poetry competition.

FLOW (the Forces Literary Organisation Worldwide) for All is dedicated to offering assistance to those who have suffered from the effects of war, especially the suffering shared by servicemen and women, their relatives and their friends.

Proceeds from the sale of this book will be used to support the work of FLOW for All, helping them to become a registered charity and to employ counsellors for those in need of care and support.

For more information please visit the following websites:
flowforall.org
flowsforum.com
forcespoetry.com
forcesstories.com

FLOW for All patron Dame Vera Lynn DBE
(Image © Giles Penfound)

Published in paperback by Silverwood Books 2009

www.silverwoodbooks.co.uk

Copyright © FLOW for All 2009

The right of FLOW for All to be identified as the authors of this work has been asserted by them in accordance with the Copyright, Designs and Patents Act 1988.

All rights reserved. No part of this publication may be reproduced, stored in a retrieval system, or transmitted in any form or by any means, electronic, mechanical, photocopying, recording or otherwise, without prior permission of the copyright holder.

ISBN 978-1-906236-25-0

British Library Cataloguing in Publication Data
A CIP catalogue record for this book is available from the British Library

Set in 11pt Bembo by SilverWood Books

POEMS OF THE POPPIES

POETRY ANTHOLOGY – VOLUME 1

from

FLOW for All

The Forces Literary Organisation Worldwide

Also available from www.silverwoodbooks.co.uk

Voices of the Poppies – An Anthology Of Poetry
(introduced by Dame Vera Lynn)

Stories of the Poppies – A Short Story Collection Volume 1

Please exercise caution
as some of the poems in this collection may be considered
unsuitable for younger readers.

Introduction

Mac Macdonald – co-founder FLOW for All

Welcome to the new poetry anthology from The Forces Literary Organisation Worldwide for All (FLOW for All).

Our initial organisation, Forces Poetry, was set up in 2005. As we grew we attracted not just poems but stories as well and so Forces Stories was born and FLOW for All was created to become the front of house organisation.

Our aim is to support those who suffer from the effects of war, and to offer a place online where anyone could come to freely express their emotions. Little did we know that within four years we'd be running competitions and publishing volumes of poetry and short stories!

Our first competitions were opened in April 2009 and ran for four months. Two competitions ran alongside each other – one accepting submissions of poetry, the other short stories. We received a consistently high standard of entries covering a range of subjects, and all entries were posted on either Forces Poetry or Forces Stories. There were no official judges; stories and poems were selected for the published collection in the most democratic way – by encouraging all visitors to vote for their favourite story or poem. The top seventy poems made it into *Poems of the Poppies* and the top twenty stories are to be published in *Stories of the Poppies*.

Reading the entries, visitors to the forums met a wonderful cast of characters and nationalities, spent time in a variety of locations and eras, and experienced an array of emotions. Some poems were uplifting, some touched on conflict and war, others reflected on loss and human dignity. Poets had written from their hearts, and this gave them the ability to reach out and touch the hearts of others.

FLOW for All would like to thank everyone who submitted their work to this year's competition and everyone who voted. Special mention should go to the moderators of flowsforums.com, who helped everything run so smoothly in spite of the occasional technical hiccup – thank you for your dedication and for giving so freely of your time.

And finally, congratulations to the seventy poets whose work makes up this year's wonderful anthology.

Thank you for purchasing this book and therefore helping us to "light up the darkness".

Mac Macdonald
2009

Contents

Some Mother's Son	17
Yesterday's News	18
Retired From The Royal Tank Regiment	19
Not Forgotten	21
Every Cloud Has A Silver Lining	22
Thank You	24
Empty Teacups	25
Shot At Dawn By Default	27
We'll Meet Again	29
The Gurkhas Betrayed	32
Long Lost Tears	35
Every Day I Kill	36
D Day	37
Return To Flanders Fields	38
We're So Proud Of You	40
After Math	45
A Helping Hand	46
Mekong Delta 1967	48
Helmand	49
War Cries	50
I Am A Warrior	52
Merchant Navy	54
Innocent Trapped Within Gaza Strip	56
All Clear	57
I Dreamed A Dream	58
Just A Common Soldier	60
Life's Journey	62
Dear Brian	63
Tom Hunter	64
Shining Angel	66
The Patrol	68
Lotus	70
Dear Lord	71
White Flowers	72
Ode To A Serving Soldier	73

Scared	74
Desert War	75
The Crowd	76
Heavens Gate	77
The Poetry Reading	79
The Dawn	80
Contentment	82
Let History Not Repeat Itself	83
Beach	84
Behind The Razor Wire	85
Grumpy Old Man	86
For My Warrior Poet	87
Six Months Later	88
The Common Soldier	89
They Call It Victory	91
Why Do I Feel So Guilty?	92
Advice From An Old Warrior	93
Letters Home	94
Marching Song	95
Nice One Harry	98
Uncle Jack	100
The 11th Hour	101
Picking Petals	104
I Want To Be A Soldier	106
Winter Already Old	107
My Light	108
The Trench	110
Laughter To Tears	112
No More!	113
Somebody Somewhere	116
Dear Mr Read	118
Brief Encounter	120
Snapshots Of War	122
He Said	123
Info	125
Too Many Times	126
Blue	127

Foreword

Major-General Tim Cross CBE

The poems contained in this little book sit within the best traditions of war poetry and writing. Challenging and moving in equal measure they provide a window into the individual hearts and minds of just some of those who are living with the consequences of having been caught up in the sorts of wars and battles that many believed we would never be involved in again.

The vast majority of the soldiers that I commanded over the years were not just good people – they and their families were quite simply some of the most impressive people I ever met. From fighting their way into places like Iraq and Afghanistan, to patrolling the streets on counter-insurgency operations around the world, they responded with humanity and humour to whatever faced them. And far from being unthinking automatons, keen for a fight and uncaring of the consequences, they asked serious questions and felt deeply about what they were engaged in.

For many of them, the military is the one place where they find true friendship. But along with the memories of the good times, when they individually and collectively made a tremendous difference to the lives of those caught up in the maelstrom of war, they carry too the memories of the violence and the failures – and, in particular, the memories of the death and injury of those friends.

For some – indeed many – the experiences build and enhance their confidence. But many struggle to come to terms with all that they have seen and heard – and some are locked in depression and loneliness. Abandoned by those that sent them off to war, all too often they and their families are left alone to face up to the events that they have been through, in a world that has little or no comprehension of what they have experienced.

Being able to talk and write about what they have experienced is a part of the healing process. So, read what they have to say with pride – and as you do, please build inside yourself a resolve not to forget this new generation of soldiers and their loved ones who have been, and continue to be, at the front line of dealing with humanity's failings.

Major-General Tim Cross CBE
2009

Foreword

Ruth Rayment

On the 4th August 2004 my nuclear family changed forever. The idea of what a family should be – a mum, dad, sister and brother – was abruptly ended and I have no doubt it is a day I shall never forget.

My brother, Pte Christopher Gordon Rayment, died through an accidental death in Iraq, Al Amarah at 11.30am. By 5.30pm that day we had two people from Woolwich, Royal Artillery Barracks inform my family of Christopher's death. It was almost like the clock had stopped for us; my family had suddenly become a statistic, my brother another name on the list of many who had already died in the name of terrorism.

After Christopher died, as his youngest sister I struggled to deal with his death, as did many people in my family. This was my first death, and the whole process of grief was completely overwhelming beyond all words. I went through every stage of grief imaginable and at one point I wondered if I were ever going to feel the same again. The only way I can describe it is being stuck down a huge hole and not being able to climb to the top to get out.

Then just when I feared there would never be an answer or resolve to my emotions and the way I was feeling, I discovered the Forces Poetry website. I began writing poetry, something I had a passion for at the age of thirteen. Now at sixteen years of age I found my only comfort in my brother's death was writing about him or my new found faith, which also gave me the inner strength to pull through a traumatic event in my life.

When I'm writing poetry, even to this day, five years on from Christopher's death, I feel like I'm in a whole new world, a different element, and everything that is within my mind pours out and is formed into yet another poem. When I'm writing I think about the pain, the loss, the anger and the torment my mind went through, and then I return back to reality and see what these emotions have enabled me to create.

I hope this Forces Poetry Anthology will allow the readers to see what does go through the grieving minds of those soldiers, families and friends and those who have served our country. May the readers see that no truer word was said than 'what doesn't kill you, makes you stronger.'

Ruth Rayment
2009

POEMS OF THE POPPIES

POETRY ANTHOLOGY – VOLUME 1

Some Mother's Son

Brenda Maple

Remembrance Day, with poppies red
Placed upon the Tomb,
November's rain to mourn the Dead,
In shrouds of mist and gloom.

All our fallen Soldiers, true
Are faded into dust,
Pilots brave and Sailors' crew,
Lie among the Just.

Elgar's music carries tears
When words do not convey
The futility of youth's lost years,
Blown, like leaves, away.

Every one some Mother's son,
Some sweetheart left to weep,
They bought our freedom with their blood,
We shall remembrance keep.

Yesterday's News

Written in memory of those who have fallen in Afghanistan.

Lorraine England

Once our deaths were front page news
Now our deaths are out of view
Shadowed by celebrity and credit crunch fears
Our commitment remembered in future years?
Ordinary men leading extraordinary lives
Separated by war from family and wives
Working alone in barren lands
In small rural villages and hot desert sands
Mortars and snipers a daily threat
From an enemy new that we've rarely met
Professional and proud, we stand side-by-side
Driven by service and sense of pride
Once our deaths were front page news
Our lives given freely despite your views
Shadowed by yours and others fears
Will you remember us in future years?
What we achieved despite all the hype
What we fought for with all our might
Will you speak proudly of what we've achieved?
For democracy; for freedom; and a foreign need?
Will you talk of our efforts with pride?
Will you pay homage at our grave sides?
Will you speak proudly to all of our sons?
Will you write honourably of what we've done?
Once our deaths were front page news
On this foreign war what are your views?
Are we only yesterday's news?

Retired From
The 2nd Royal Tank Regiment

I wrote this poem about my lover who has trouble settling back in to life after retiring from the army. To me it seems that a lot of army people struggle with this after a long period in the army and it's quite a common problem for them to be somewhat trapped and unfeeling, not relating well to civilian people, especially women.

Vicki Lines

Retired from the 2nd Royal Tank Regiment,
my identity has gone,
Pangs of loneliness, isolation the nights are long.
I've seen my comrades wounded, fallen at my feet,
Now dumped in this no-mans land called Civilian Street.

I have fought with pride for my country and served the Queen,
Civilians could not contemplate what I have seen,
But, now not caring whether I am alive or dead,
The price of reality is messing with my head.

In the army, united, we followed every rule,
But out here it appears that everyone is a fool.
I just can't seem to settle, I move from place to place,
The same endless circle of women, face after face.

My feelings and thoughts locked away for no one to see,
Sure in the knowledge that nobody has the key.
Behind the title of tank commander I can hide,
Just as long as everything can stay trapped inside.

I have a few army friends, fags and Jameson Scotch,
Regimental medals, lighter and souvenir watch.
I keep convincing myself that is enough for me.
You will have to be a special woman to set me free.

I know this is survival; it's not life that I live,
I am empty inside; there is nothing left to give.
Only enough love for Sarah and Joshu to share,
But for anyone else I make no promise to care.

Not Forgotten

Susan Haniford

Don't worry Mum I've not forgotten my vest
Even though this foreign weather is warm.
Out here at the front I still look my best
I'm proud to take care of my new uniform.

Don't worry Mum I've not forgotten my hat
No soldier's properly prepared without one.
It's on my head sitting proud and all that
Steel is glinting brightly out here in the sun.

Don't worry Mum I've not forgotten to eat
The rations we have really are quite grand.
There's fine red wine, potatoes, fish and meat
The crockery is the finest in the land.

Don't worry Mum I've not forgotten respect
And every night, I remember to pray.
I'm always polite which I know's correct
And I ask God for good things to come our way.

Don't worry Mum I've not forgotten the date
All my mates know that I've just turned sixteen.
These fireworks for me, they really are great,
Loud and more colourful than I've ever seen.

Don't worry Mum I've not forgotten to write
But can't now; my hands are numb, my head's sore.
I'm not alone, someone's holding me tight.
Says I'm leaving, won't have to fight any more.

Don't worry Mum but I need to have a sleep
Underneath this dazzling sky of blue.
It's fine here at the front, no need to weep
I'm coming home soon and I'll be back with you.

Every Cloud Has A Silver Lining

Michelle Wendy D'Costa

It was a dream come true
I was getting married
To a soldier, to someone the nation knew
So my consent or the lack of it wasn't paid any heed

My parents were ecstatic
There only daughter was now settled
I was gifted a white floral dress of batik
In which I was lovingly nestled

The Big Day got over with astonishing speed
I miss it now
I wish it comes back; I plead
Oh! How beautiful I looked while taking the vow

He loved me much more than anyone could
Promised to buy me a new nightgown on his return
I lowered my gaze; how bashful I must have looked!
Then he kissed me goodbye, my stomach began to churn

I prayed everyday, much more than I was used to
His letters became rare
I clinged on to the few like superglue
Then suddenly they stopped, I hoped it was only a nightmare

I was worried sick
As if confirming my thoughts, I received a letter
The war had begun and so did my baby's kick
In the following months, nothing became better

The kicking continued
But not his messages
I cried myself to sleep every night in order to elude
The cruel truth that threatened my senses

He will come back, come back soon
I consoled myself now and then
When the bad news struck, it was noon
It was delivered by two uniformed men

His corpse looked forlorn
I was helpless, resigned to fate
The next day my baby was born
It was an hour late

At the age of twenty, I became a widow
Living with my husband's memory and baby
I decided to move on, away from his demise's shadow
It was difficult but I dragged along daily

Later, my son lifted the pall from my life
He swore not to follow the family's tradition
To maintain the sanity of his mother and wife
I thanked God for his intuitive decision

Thank You

The old git ROATS

I pin a poppy to my chest
I wear it with such pride
I wear it for the ones now gone
For those who fought and died

I wear it to say thank you
To those who gave their lives
To buy us all our freedom
Which in this land still thrives

To all of you who lost a friend
or loved one held so dear
I honour you as well today
And every single year

Empty Teacups

Dedicated to all parents who have suffered and who still suffer the pain and loss of a 'child'.

Jan Hedger

The knock came at night, crashing into the midnight stillness.
Pulling the bedclothes high, I encased myself in their security
Abject fear engulfing every muscle, every sinew in my body.
Dad was the one who moved, sliding bare feet into slippers
As if they were placed there in position for this very reason.
I felt his cold, tremulous hand, gently rest upon my shoulder
Just briefly; before the incessant knock sounded again.
As he clicked the bedroom door quietly, but firmly behind him
I felt an overwhelming vacuum of complete and utter emptiness
The blood draining from my heart, leaving in its wake an
echoing beat
I buried down deeper, to silence it. I am sorry Dad,
you have to go alone.
I willed myself, indeed ordered myself to return to the state
of sleep
To hide, from the compelling, waiting truth, behind tightly
shut eyes,
See the nightmare through, wake up refreshed,
to a new spring day.
A day renewed with hope, that in two weeks my boy WILL
be home!
Two weeks is nothing, for I waited twenty years for him
to be born
There came no others; he is my one pride and joy;
and still my baby.
I don't know if I did sleep, or just lay comatose into
the early hours
But daylight was filtering through the curtains when
my head obeyed,
A sudden inexplicit need to lift itself from the pillow comfort.

I thrust my arms firmly into the sleeves of a blue, corded
dressing gown,
With a belied resoluteness, that I should pull myself together,
be strong,
Go down, put the kettle on, Dad will need a cup of tea, sweet tea,
Always a comfort in a crisis, it's what they had drunk in the
other war.
My tread fell soft upon the carpeted stair, tentative and afraid,
Of the hidden truth of realisation, that awaited me;
for a mother knew.
Dad was standing looking out at the garden, where a swing
once stood
His shoulders stooped, his body collapsed, barely holding the
weight of his frame
Lost in his own pain, he didn't hear me come in, or feel my
presence in the room.
It was the teacups that did it; just three white empty teacups,
Drained by the midnight callers, leaving their mark on the
polished table.
A scream I couldn't suppress unleashed itself from the depths
of my womb
Filling the air with a grief that would never be explained
or understood.
'It's our boy, isn't it Dad. It's our boy, he's gone. My baby's gone'.
Dad caught me just before I fell, 'I know mom' he uttered with a
Strangled sob, 'I know'.

Shot At Dawn By Default

To the young and the Brave of World War I.

Tom Mcgreevy

I'm standing here alone
My back against the wall
My body is a trembling
I'm slumped, but once stood tall

My blindfold wet and cold
Sticking to my tears
I search my mind for future life
Beyond my 18 years

My knees transformed to putty
Can't support my weight
My hands tied by my Country
Which once I thought was great

They said I was a coward
They never asked me why
Court Marshalled here in secret
I know I'm going to die

I can't see what is happening
My blindfold bound so tight
The silence now is killing me
As Dawn appears from night

Get it over, get it done
Why do they make me wait ?
I really need to urinate
Can't they see my state ?

A clicking from the Rifle Bolts
A stream runs down my leg
I only have but seconds left
"Don't kill me" now I beg

The fear it makes me Vomit
The birds they start to trill
Then suddenly go quiet
The eerie Dawn stands still

The birds they sense a Death is near
Life ends right here for me
A 'Crack!' from all those rifles
In perfect harmony

Send a message to my loved ones
Don't listen, what they said
I was young and frightened
I shouldn't lie here dead

We'll Meet Again

In memory of a very good friend who is now 'upstairs'.

Annie Taylor

I remember getting hit by it
The blast it knocked me over
I think I landed on me arse
Just by the burning rover

I remember mates all rushing
To help me sort things out
I said "you stupid bastards
I'm alright" I shout

"I'm fine" I said "get off you lot"
But they fussed me just the same
Then slowly washing over me
a wave of dulling pain

Ooh that hurts I said to them
What the hell is that?
You'll be ok now matey
This jab will hold it back

Only then it dawned on me
Their faces said it all
It wasn't just a flesh wound
I was heading for the fall

I felt all kind of woozy
And then all nice and calm
Then Sandy knelt beside me
And gently held my arm

I saw him glance at Murdock
Trying to hide his fear
He knew that he was losing me
And then I saw his tears

I squeezed his hand and smiled at him
I told him not to cry
That I loved him like a brother
And whispered my goodbye

He couldn't hold it in no more
His tears and rage released
He screamed at god and everyone
Make this killing cease

And as I left them weeping
Their hearts in pain for me
I slipped away so quietly
I wish that they could see

I drifted slowly off to sleep
I couldn't feel the heat
I didn't smell or ache at all
Now this is really neat

I woke to see him staring
The warmest smile I've seen
He looked into my heart he did
As if it was a dream

He asks me what I wanted
"are the wife and kids ok"?
He smiles and points just down below
I see them plain as day

I know they really want me home
And wish we weren't apart
and though no longer with them
I'll live on in their hearts

We walk on through and there they are
Family, friends and more
And as they cheer and welcome me
He guards the open door

So if you've lost a loved one
Then weep for them no more
As they are safe and sound up here
With him to guard the door

We'll meet again…

The Gurkhas Betrayed

Here is a poem about the shameful treatment of the Gurkhas and the hypocrisy of the Government.

Finn

We fought and we fell
for your country
over two hundred years
we have served

and through
all the wars
and the battles
our loyalty
never has swerved.

We fought and we died
for your country
we
never questioned the cost

Ten
times five thousand comrades
Ten
times five thousand lost.

The bugles called out
at their gravesides
to show that you honoured
them all

that you valued the service
they gave you
those brothers who heeded
your call.

Over six thousand medals
you gave them
for the courage
they brought to your cause

Two
hundred thousand
brave soldiers
who fought by your side
in your wars.
Yes Bugles
spoke out at their gravesides
The flags they dipped in salute

If they
knew
how you valued their honour
their voices each one would be mute.

For
though we have
died for your country
it's a place without
welcome to give

by your rules we are caught
our service too short

to a land
where you won't
let us live.

Yes it seems that the service we gave you
was different in kind and degree
from our comrades the commonwealth soldiers
whose entry you each guarantee.

You're besmirching
your name
and your honour
with rules that
are petty and small

disdaining the name of the Gurkhas
the fighters who answered your call.

Honour the name of the Gurkhas
all those who fought and who died

welcome the soldiers who served you
whose duty was given with pride.

Long Lost Tears

Peter Southern

I held the rabbit in my arms today and cuddled it
as it was put to sleep
He looked so peaceful, no more pain. As I stroked him I started
to weep.
In years gone by I had been to war, killed, and seen friends die
I stood there with tears running down my face, just a little rabbit
so why, oh why did I cry?

Perhaps those tears that I wept today while stroking those
floppy ears
Were those long lost tears that I had been holding in for far too
many years?
In times of war there's no time to cry, no time to show you care
And of all the things I hold inside, there are still those I fear
to share

Every Day I Kill

Alex Roissetter

I killed a man today,
It happened in my waking,
I looked in the mirror and there he was,
His heart forever breaking.

I killed a child today,
He was in my head playing,
And in three ranks at attention standing,
Into the past he fades praying.

I killed my love today,
It was in my heart singing,
But in my rifles report it fled,
And in its place it leaves a stinging.

I killed a soldier this afternoon,
It was when I took off those clothes,
And when I sit and talk with my friends,
The ghosts of the child and man in me flows.

D Day

James Tattersall

They went through hell but they kept going.
As they got out of landing craft bullets came at them.
Nearly all of them got killed.
From this day they will be remembered.
Only a few survived.

Return To Flanders Fields

Holly Kernott

And while the landscape has changed and planes now fly overhead
We will not forget the sacrifice you made,
Soldiers: Forever young, forever brave
Silenced by death.
Who laid down their lives in Flanders Fields

Countless raindrops have fallen since then,
But it has not made us forget,
Despite the passing of the years,
Tears are still wept, falling like the rain.

Those who thought that the war they fought
Would be the war to end all wars
United in their vision to protect the nation
Selfless acts indeed
Whose journey ended in Flanders Fields.

Today, a new generation
Stand with the people of the years gone past
To pay their respects to the men who perhaps found peace,
Comforted that they did not die in vain
But battled for a new generation so they could be free
And live in peace again

With the poppy still burning red
A lasting reminder to all
Of the courage and kindness and bravery
Of the men who gave their all.

Words cannot portray
The gratitude we have for the men of yesterday
The poppy's message is quite clear when worn,
And speaks more proficiently than any words could say.

The silence on the eleventh hour,
Pays tribute and calls out across the years
Back to those fields, where the wind softly whistles, with a message to impart
So the men who fell in battle may rest peacefully at last

For the generations are united
And time and age depart
And the message from the new generation is 'thank you'
'Thank you with all our hearts.'

We're So Proud Of You

My son is currently serving in Iraq on his first tour, he is only 19 and strange as it may seem, he is loving every minute of it. I wrote this poem with him in mind but also to every parent who has a son currently out on operations… this could be them. It is in support of all our serving soldiers and although it is written around a male soldier, it in no way undermines the hard work and determination that our female soldiers do and it is in respect of these brave young women as well as the men.

Michaela Turner

From birth to age five
His life's just begun
The world is his oyster
Full of laughter and fun
He's playing at soldiers
Hiding behind trees
Ducking and diving
Scuffing his knees

From six to age twelve
He's off with his mates
Playing out of sight now
From the garden gates
He's up to all sorts
But nothing too bad
Just being mischievous
A typical lad

A teenager now
The arguments begin
He's pushing the limits
He thinks he can win
Parents know nothing
They've never lived

His words can be hurtful
But we always forgive

Then the day comes
For choices to take
Of his chosen career
What a decision to make
"What shall I do?"
"What can I be?"
"I want to choose something
To make you proud of me"

He thinks and he thinks
Till his mind is sore
Then suddenly one day
Opportunity knocks on the door
A television advert
Come take our test
To see if you are ready
To be one of THE BEST

"That's it I've got it,
That's what I'll be!"
"I'll be a soldier,
I'll serve my country"
So it's off to Scotland
He tries his best
To make the selection
Ahead of the rest

Then the day comes
When the letter arrives
He opens it carefully
There's hope in his eyes
"It's yes, YES I've made it
They want me in"
"And they've given me a date
When I can begin"

We're so proud of you son,
We knew you'd get through
Your dreams of being a soldier,
Have finally come true
So much training to do son,
Far away from home
But we'll always be there for you love,
On the end of the phone

A whole new world now
Has opened for you
Just keep on trying
You'll make it through
It will not be easy
The training you'll do
But it's the only way
To make a Man out of you

Pass out day comes
He's standing there proud
And looking for his family
Amongst the crowd
The ceremony begins
You can't help but cry
So proud of your soldier
As he passes by

Then he's off to Battalion
To his chosen career
He receives word of his posting
This you don't want to hear
You knew it would happen
But you didn't want to face
That he's to be posted
To a sandy place

The day then comes
To say your goodbyes
You're trying to hide
The tears in your eyes
And so it begins
Months full of worry
You hope and you pray
They pass by in a hurry

A few weeks pass by
You've not even heard
A single phone call
Not a single word
You can't help but worry
You don't sleep at night
And there on the news
What a terrible sight

The base has been hit
It's been 'raining' all night
Your worries and fears
Turn to panic and fright
You close your eyes
And hold back the tears
As you reminisce
On his childhood years

You think of those soldiers
Who've been wounded or fallen
And you pray for peace now
For those poor lives that are stolen
You think of the families
Of the heartache they bear
And you cannot help it
Their sorrow you share

You pray for his safety
For his mates as well
They shouldn't be there
In that place of hell
Then at last he's calling
From out of the blue
You thank God they're ok
Your prayers they've come true

He'll be home soon now
From that sandy place
And you cannot wait
To see his smiling face
When the day comes
He seems much older
But you hug and you kiss him
Your brave little soldier

So to all of our soldiers
Wherever you are
We stand and salute you
Our shining stars
You fight for our freedom
Being honest and true
And we just want to say that
WERE SO PROUD OF YOU

After Math

Mark Dron

Sun-Bleached bones, stretch across the dust.
In cloudless skies of dazzling white the Vultures circle
echoes of the fallen,
uniformed spectres fade,
the shades of the lost,
haunt these blasted fields.
Steel creatures lie sides ruptured,
twisted and torn.
Blistered and blackened,
paint peels away exposing the rusting hearts.
Figures in khaki,
shattered, battered,
draped like plastic dolls
warped and melted in blazing heat,
the Vultures soar,
picking over broken bones.
Black muzzles point skywards,
Scorched and rusting,
burnt metal,
blistered,
blasted,
Silence hangs like Cancer,
swollen and bloated it creeps.
In the bone-white skies,
The Vultures circle.

A Helping Hand

Mac Macdonald

Blinking faintly just a spot
a distant light or maybe not
Is it them come back for more
or is it mates in teams of four

I crawl a bit to hide my form
and nearer still the light comes on
Nearer yet to me it gets
I check my rifle prepare for threat

Then quietly a voice I hear
"come on son, have no fear"
A friendly voice thank god for that
I prepare to move from where I'm sat

The voice gets nearer almost here
I know I'm saved I lose my fear
I see a person just ahead
ready to move (my legs feel dead)

Now I see him now he's here
his face I know but still I peer
"I came to get you don't be scared
your job is done, you've been spared"

I take his hand my legs now work
I stand beside him and start to smirk
I see some others coming through
there's old man Stan and Connor too

And as I walk with him a while
I see more mates and start to smile
But all these mates weren't they dead?
Have I been injured lost my head?

How obvious it soon became
Mohamed, Allah, Christ (just names)
Standing there with all my squad
The hand I took was that of God

Mekong Delta 1967

Jim Brosnan

A hot sultry May breeze
provides little comfort
from the scorching night
temperatures – the jungle
humidity. I scan treetops
for creeping or hunched
silhouettes in the shadow
of this full moon. Nearby
cypress and mangrove
provide such cover. Ten
feet away a branch bristles.
Desire for a Lucky Strike,
a deep drag of nicotine,
must wait. A canvas of stars
twinkle in this midnight hour
as jet fighters rumble overhead.
In the distant mountains
artillery shells pop
like Fourth of July fireworks.
Static radio transmission
provides no coordinates.
I yawn, calculate the minutes
left on my night watch.
I am exhausted.
We had drilled all day
in the beating sun.

Helmand

John Hawkhead

Night on the cold plain,
invisible sands lift,
peripheral shadows stir,

space between light and dark
shrouding secrets;
old trades draped grey.

Here too poppies fall,
petals blown on broken ground
seeds scattered on stone

and this bright bloom,
newly cropped,
leaves pale remains

fresh lines cut;
the old sickle wind
sharp as yesterday.

War Cries

H.M. Gruendler-Schierloh

In the darkened city people listened with fear
to the roaring of enemy planes drawing near
to fulfill their mission
of some political vision
as with deadly precision
they blew buildings and bodies asunder.
And the sky grew dark with eerie smoke,
eerie smoke filled the sky,
as in the struggle for human rights
the right to live went under;
> the right to live it went under
> with buildings and bodies blown asunder.

Defending ideologies that had been instilled,
soldier turned upon soldier and killed
in the mindless state
of impersonal hate
of one whose fate
it is to see bodies in agony writhe.
And the sky smelled strongly of rancid blood
the smell of blood filled the sky
when to save the world for democracy
democratic ideals were compromised;
> democratic ideals they were compromised
> in the bodies that in agony writhed.

Metal buzzards approached, preparing to dive,
as women and children ran for their life
with no place to hide,
one more ugly side
of the terrible plight
of a people driven from their native land.
And the sky resounded with helpless cries,
helpless cries filled the sky
as in the name of justice

injustice gained the upper hand;
>　injustice gained the upper hand
>　for a people driven from their native land.

To destroy some ominous military installation
and ammunition depots of another nation
was the official goal.
But what about the toll
exerted from the soul
of a slaughtered child by the wayside?
And the sky hung heavy in black despair,
black despair filled the sky
as in the war for humanity
the essence of humanity died;
>　the essence of humanity it died
>　in a slaughtered child by the wayside.

I Am A Warrior

John Sinclair

I am a warrior
Tall and proud
My hand is my guide
For my sword and my shield

I will not yield
I will fight to my last
I am a warrior
Who will have a glorious past?

My clan chieftain the leader
Wise and bold
He has led us to victory
So many times untold
Great stories through the centuries
Will have to be told

I am draped in my tartan
A glorious sight
No wonder the enemy always takes fright
The sound of the pipes
To steady the nerves
A glorious sound
Nowhere else to be found

We move forward into battle
Under banners and flags
This looks to be the best rammy
We ever will have

The battle is over
The day has been won
Let the celebrations unfold
There are battle stories to be told

My tartan is bloodied
But I feel no pain
I am a warrior
Tall and proud

Merchant Navy

Kerry Dainty

A war, a convoy, a letter through the door,
A wife that is a wife no more
Her children are called away from school
To be broken the news so terribly cruel

"Your father has sailed to a distant land
And can not be reached by human hand
No more shall we meet him upon the quay
He can not come back to you or to me"

Some days later, when tears have passed
Her children asleep and quiet at last
She sits down to wish of one more goodbye
And to ponder and puzzle and ask merely why?

The warships guard the convoys tight,
Prepared to stand, prepared to fight.
But they are not who the foe will attack.
They hunt the ones that cannot fight back.

"My husband has sailed to a distant land,
Following orders of higher command,
He sails his ship on a distant sea
Never again to dock on an English quay"

Who will remember the warships and crew?
The soldiers in trenches, the men who flew?
All will remember the forces of men,
Who left, never to return again.

But who will remember the brave men of sea
Whose ships were unarmed and could only flee?
Who shouldered the burden of feeding their land,
In ships with conditions fit for the damned

I will remember, with poppy and voice
To tell of the merchant ships and of their choice.
The trawler, the cargo ship, fishing boats too,
I remember their sacrifice and say Thank You

Innocent Trapped Within The Gaza Strip

Sophie Meads

Unity undefined. Unapproachable
Indistinctive boundaries of innocence
Tied unwillingly, born into this rubble
Of wars reluctantly chained with conscience

Unavoidably so interested
Morality low, familiarity
Inevitable, relentlessly led
Comprehension too far, lack clarity.

Acquaintance with this place, not only through
Intrigue, misunderstanding the danger
As well as the intended cause, but you
Must fight for it anyway, this stranger

For survival instincts drive you, not me
To chaos running through pages of history

All Clear

A. R. Lewis

Two words,
That mean so much,
To all who live trusting,
To hear the consultant say them.
ALL CLEAR.

I Dreamed A Dream

Peter D Bruffell

Last night I dreamed a beautiful dream
That I went f or a walk with God,
We strolled along a bright sunbeam
Eating chips and battered cod.

He told me that He loved me,
And said, 'He knew I loved Him too.'
He showed me things I wanted to see
Like how He 'made the sky so blue.'

I asked Him, "how mankind was doing?"
But He didn't answer me,
He wasn't very happy
And that was plain to see.

He told me, 'to be careful,
Along the path of life,'
He said, "don't be resentful,"
And to, 'take care of my wife.'

I asked Him, 'How was Jesus?'
He said, "He will be fine
But his wounds have not yet healed,
Even after all this time."

As we walked along the leafy lane,
I tired, so He carried me,
We then sat down, within the shade,
Of a beautiful old oak tree!

I held His hand so tightly
As He cuddled up to me,
His heart was love and comfort,
So I asked to, 'stay for eternity?'

But He replied that, 'I must go
To carry on with my life,'
And as I woke, from my dream
I snuggled up closely to my wife.

I told her that, 'I loved her,'
She said, 'she loved me too.'
I then felt a glow, deep inside
And I knew that my dream was true.

Just A Common Soldier

(A Soldier Died Today)

A. Lawrence Vaincourt

He was getting old and paunchy and his hair was falling fast,
And he sat around the Legion, telling stories of the past
Of a war that he had fought in and the deeds that he had done,
In his exploits with his buddies; they were heroes, every one.

And tho' sometimes, to his neighbours, his tales became a joke,
All his Legion buddies listened, for they knew whereof
he spoke.
But we'll hear his tales no longer for old Bill has passed away,
And the world's a little poorer, for a soldier died today.

He will not be mourned by many, just his children and his wife,
For he lived an ordinary and quite uneventful life.
Held a job and raised a family, quietly going his own way,
And the world won't note his passing,
though a soldier died today.

When politicians leave this earth, their bodies lie in state,
While thousands note their passing and proclaim that they
were great.
Papers tell their whole life stories, from the time that they
were young,
But the passing of a soldier goes unnoticed and unsung.

Is the greatest contribution to the welfare of our land
A guy who breaks his promises and cons his fellow man?
Or the ordinary fellow who, in times of war and strife,
Goes off to serve his Country and offers up his life?

A politician's stipend and the style in which he lives
Are sometimes disproportionate to the service that he gives.
While the ordinary soldier, who offered up his all,
Is paid off with a medal and perhaps, a pension small.

It's so easy to forget them for it was so long ago,
That the old Bills of our Country went to battle, but we know
It was not the politicians, with their compromise and ploys,
Who won for us the freedom that our Country now enjoys.

Should you find yourself in danger, with your enemies at hand,
Would you want a politician with his ever-shifting stand?
Or would you prefer a soldier, who has sworn to defend
His home, his kin and Country and would fight until the end?

He was just a common soldier and his ranks are growing thin,
But his presence should remind us we may need his like again.
For when countries are in conflict, then we find the
soldier's part
Is to clean up all the troubles that the politicians start.

If we cannot do him honour while he's here to hear the praise,
Then at least let's give him homage at the ending of his days.
Perhaps just a simple headline in a paper that would say,
Our Country is in mourning, for a soldier died today.

Life's Journey

Dedicated to David Murray

David, from Carlisle, died at a roadside bombing. He was nineteen. For more details of David's life please access 'Tributes' at The Evening News & Star.

Robert Carson

Loyal son, and brother, a good friend too
We feel such pain at losing you.
Yours, was the ultimate human cost
What could console us for your loss?
Your death would stain the soil with blood
Our eyes have wept with tears of love...
Such happy memories we have known
Of one, who died so far from home.
'Rest, now, at peace our precious son
Your journey through this life is done.
Within this earth -one sleeps at rest
Whose name's forever on our breaths.'

Dear Brian...

Christie Bowman

It has been almost three months
Since you went away
To be a good soldier
And find your way.

As I sit and watch TV
The pain in my heart is so strong
I think about the day
That I have been waiting for, for so long.

The day that you will come home
And kiss me on my cheek
The day that you are back
So I won't feel so weak.

The day that you hold my hand
And tell me how much you love me
The day that we just sit around
And I wait for you to hug me.

The day that I can see your dimples
And look at your beautiful smile
The day that I can be with you
And not have to wait for such a long while.

This is the day, you see
That will make the Army life worthwhile
This is the day for me
To great you with a warm smile.

I love you and miss you dearly.
Be safe and take care and I will see you soon.
Love always, Christie.

Tom Hunter

Brian Morton

You're a hero Tom Hunter, so all the boys say
You're a hero I know, in your own quiet way.

You've seen plenty of action, you've been through the mill,
you were there in the battle on Tumbledown Hill.
You were there when young Frankie stood up and got shot,
spun round by the bullet that opened his gut.
You were the one put the field dressing on
and held him and watched as he died in the sun.
You were there once before, in the fight at Goose Green
when you saw good men die and you heard young boys scream.
Now what do you say when they ask about wars
"Did you kill one or two? Do you have any scars?"
Do you mention the wounds in your head every night
and of waking with knuckles tight clenched screaming white.

You're a hero Tom Hunter, so all the boys say,
you're a hero I know, in your own quiet way.
You can tell them the truth, you can tell them it all,
or do as you do and say nothing at all.

You were there in The Gulf when the call came once more
fighting other men's children in other men's wars.
You were there in the sand with the sun on your back
when the sky filled with hate and the daylight went black.
You were there when the beaches were covered in oil
when the quiet gulf waters seemed almost to boil,
when the lights of the world seemed dismal and dull
when we all saw that truck and the black staring skull.

You're a hero Tom Hunter, so all the boys say,
you're a hero I know, in your own quiet way.
You can tell them the truth, you can tell them it all,
or do as you do and say nothing at all.

Now that you're home and the fighting's all past
its all put behind you and you're safe at last.
But each time you look at your own teenage son
you remember the boys that forever are gone.
The ones that you left, who fought and who died,
the ones who are dying tonight in your mind.

You're a hero Tom Hunter, so all the boys say
You're a hero I know, in your own quiet way.
You can tell them the truth, you can tell them it all,
or do as you do and say nothing at all.

Shining Angel

In honour of all QA's and VAD's.

Sheila Weekes

For God's sake, don't judge her as she is now,
she was once a most elegant beauty.
All the young men would salute in awe
as serving her country was her duty.

She never had a home or family of her own
there just never seemed to be the time.
When the day came she hung up her uniform
she thought she was well past her prime.

She knew life like most women never know,
at the front line battlefields of war,
where bombs were blasting, smoke and terror,
she was right up there at the fore.

She would stay for hours through the night
to light a cigarette or hold a trembling hand.
Way past when her nursing duties were over,
in some strange, foreign, bombed out land.

She new the screams of those limbless or blind,
she wrote letters to their dearest kin.
Held many like frightened babies in the night
until the early morning sun crept back in.

For all the wives that she pretended to be,
talking soothing words for hours on end
just to make them hang on, have the will,
so their poor broken bodies could mend.

Now she ends her days in a nursing home,
just a shrivelled little lady with silver hair.
One of our own military, shining angels,
reliving her memories in a big armchair.

The Patrol

This is dedicated to all our armed forces personnel serving in Afghanistan.

Ros Williams

As I patrol this dusty track
I find myself thinking back
To soldiers who were here before
And bravely fought in this merciless war
The Taliban hide all around
In the hills and under ground
And as I slowly pass you by
I see the look in your eye
Who you are, I do not know
Are you friend or are you foe
Do your children do your spying
Will you sing and dance as I lay dying
From your bullet in my back
Or explosion from a mortar attack
Or will you invite my friends and me
Into your homes to take some tea

As I patrol this dusty track
I find myself looking back
Over my shoulder to check and see
That all my mates are still with me
Then all at once that thunderous sound
As explosions blast all around
And as I dive to take my cover
A mortar explodes, and then another
Adrenaline flows, I have no fear
My hands are steady, my sight is clear

In the distance I see a figure
I take my aim and squeeze the trigger
And as insurgents fall from their place
Others flee, without trace
They run and hide far away
Returning to fight another day

Lotus

Ankita Saxena

The wind will breathe over every ocean, but one will begin
the tidal wave,
Which will never stop blowing out its neutral coloured misery,
Who would think that what fills our body, could drown
our heart,
That the world we live in every day can suddenly turn
to a battlefield,
That the mould which we were created from is then
what destroys us,
Who would think that anything good can get out of bad and
bad put together,
That dazzling pink petals could unfurl out of a filthy pond,
That a lotus is born out of a foundation, not even a thorn
would live in,
No clear water reflection – its future is muddy – but the goal
clear,
It displays the true colours not the mirror image, the mirage
of one's self,
For real success measures the difference between the reactants
and the products,
The dirty pond and the dancing lotus, the homeless boy and the
leading actor
For when you look in that shining mirror – you are not seeing
the lotus,
But a polished glass panel, giving you the colours, but not
setting the scene,
Giving you the picture, but not the whole image, giving you
the pretty flower,
But not the struggles it has fought, to make that flower, the
most beautiful of all!

Dear Lord

Ruth Rayment

Please give me the strength I need to make it through the days
Through the nights that seem so endlessly long
And yet the dawn of day rises so quick
Allow me the serenity to move on with the gliding days
Not to be bitter, but to deal with the consequences of life
Please give me hope, to create a new day
And a chance to reminiscence on him.... the one I so dearly miss
Dear Lord, Allow me to accept the things of which I know I cannot change… Amen!

White Flowers

Roberta Coelho

Little children lying dead
Like white flowers stained deepest red
Heaven knows what went through their heads
While their parents watched with dread
Listening for every tread.

Now little girls can't use their charms
Nor walk down the aisle on their father's arm
And what about the little boys?
They will no longer need their toys

With every bullet and every bomb
Their parents' dreams are dead and gone
How will they ever carry on?

Ode To A Serving Soldier

Susan Pullar

A soldier stood on the corner of the street,
watching the world go by,
He wonders who, next he will meet, or if he's next in line to die,
He stands there not for the fun of his health,
instead he's gambling with his life,
Wondering what fate has in store for him, or if he'll ever again
see his loving wife.

His folks at home all think he's grand, but the Irish have
different ides,
The Irish are the enemy, the people the soldier fears,
At last another soldier relieves him, so he can go back
where he can relax,
For just a short while, but be ready, for sudden attack.

A soldier is always on "Stand by", he must always be "Alert",
Ready to go out without notice, and perhaps have to lie
in the dirt,
Or lie low in some field, on an O.P, with little or no
radio contact,
Then he wonders why the hell, he ever signed the
Army contract.

His idea was not to be a hero, when he signed on the
dotted line,
Not to be fighting in Ireland, because it's just a complete
waste of time,
No thanks will he get for the heartache, for witnessing
carnage and pain,
No relief he will he feel when it's time to go home,
Because he knows he will be back again and again!

SCARED

I wrote these poem many years ago when I was going through a rough period in my life. I feel that many
people either serving or their families, will find some comfort from them, as I tried to put my belief that the people we love are always with us even when they aren't there, alive or dead. I've spent the majority of the 2 and a half years that i've known my husband, away from him, so I know how hard it can be to be seperated. I hope others get some sort of understanding from these poems.

Kayleigh Carey

I'm scared I'll never see you again,
That you'll leave me all alone.
I need you in my life,
For you are my guiding star.

I'm scared you'll leave without,
Saying goodbye.
That I'll say something hurtful,
And you'll go away disappointed.

I'm scared I'll fail,
Your understanding,
Your trust,
Your hopes in me.

I'm scared I'll,
Lose you forever,
And I'll never hold you close,
Or tell you that I love you again.

Desert War

Jean M Hendrickson

sunday death
sandbox tanks
cinnamon sands
shivering shadows
simmering mirages
shimmering shapes
sharp grief
stop
before one more spirit
is weaned from it's body

The Crowd

Sammy

Terrified eyes stare through the windscreen
from a body already dead but unaware.

The crowd presses in.

A helicopter hovers overhead,
so often the angel of mercy, now filled with impotent rage.

The crowd presses in

And two friends leave the world.

Heavens Gate

Albert Forsyth

Up there above the windy sky
a million miles or more
is a world where every soul is sent
in thru a narrow door

They are counted as they enter
and entered on a roll
to ensure that they have made it
every single soul

Then one by one they are asked
where they would like to be
in the land of milk and honey
by a crystal clear blue sea

And so forever they are rested
no fear or pain to bear
just peace and pure tranquility
where home is anywhere

forever in gods bosom
they have done their worldly deed
and now with family and friends
form part of heavens breed

And as angels spread their wings
and the heavenly choir begins
our souls are cleansed forever
of all our earthly sins

The Poetry Reading

Paddy Slevin

I went to a reading last Saturday week,
Of poetry, prose and of verse.
For the lass that I love is a poetry fan.
Some things, I suppose, could be worse.

The poet in charge was an odd-looking cove.
With blue-tinted specs on his nose,
And a pink chiffon scarf tied tight 'round his neck.
For added effect I suppose.

This soirée was held in a room at The Bull.
A place of some doubtful repute.
Where T-shirts prevailed, and I swear I smelt puff.
I felt over-dressed in my suit.

Chief poet stood up to announce the first turn
"Some poetry sapphic this time".
He droned on and on, with 'is dark gloomy poem,
And never once got it to rhyme.

With a pint in his hand, and froth on his 'tash,
And his free hand scratching his groin.
'E told of King Bill and some Fenian lads,
Who'd had a big scrap on the Boyne.

Next blue-specs comes back, with a grin for my lass.
Smiling, and saying he'd treat her,
"To frolics and fun, and tales tenderly told,
In clear am-phi-bra-chic meter".

A woman was perched on the edge of a stool,
In jeans with some holes in the knee.
"There was a young lady of Warwick" she starts.
Seemed just like a Lim'rick to me.

Then some soldiers came in, from a room next door.
And asked "Can we join in the fun?"
They did "Eskimo Nell" and old "Piddlin' Pete"
Then encored with "Nelly the Nun".

Poor poetry bloke, he was getting quite miffed.
Miff showing all over his mush.
For people were cheering and clapping their hands,
And poet kept shouting for hush.

With a shrug and a grin, the poet gave in.
He'd lost all sense of decorum
As folks thanked the lads for kindly performing,
This forces poetry for 'em.

The night was not all a resounding success.
Me drinking strong ale by the yard.
At chucking-out time I quite suddenly found,
My lass had gone home. With the bard!

The Dawn

On the 27th July 2009 my wife Debbie was diagnosed with breast cancer. We were all shocked and upset and we have all started on this new journey together and this is the story so far…

Mac Macdonald

July twenty seventh two thousand and nine
A mammogram check, well worth the time
I wait in the car so I don't have to pay
Then Debs made that call on her mobile to say

I might have the cancer, (I heard her voice shake)
The seconds took minutes, please let me awake?
I leapt from the car and went to her side
I found her and held her together we cried

The shock was intense the disbelief real
We sat in our bubble unsure how to feel
We then had to wait, go back in and see
Were they correct or were we now free

We sat there outside as we waited to hear
The news we all think will never come near
We went in the room and they said all the words
We thanked them and left them and set off homewards

And then to our children we now had to go
To tell them the news letting bravery show
Deb told our son and he held her so tight
Our rock on that day and he said that we'd fight

I went to get Heather and tell her the news
Her work said no problem forget all the rules
She came out of work and she sat by my side
She got such a shock, we hugged and we cried

The worst of the feelings that hit me that day
Was the fear in Debs eyes, "I'm frightened" she'd say
I couldn't defend her, I couldn't protect
How do I fight what I can not affect?

My Debbie is wonderful sweet and so kind
A friend of all people none nicer you'll find
So why did God do this why did he allow
The cancer to visit my girl and right now

I don't understand and I don't want to know
I'm angry I'm frightened but can't let it show
My upbringing said that men are so strong
I feel my heart breaking so that theory's wrong

★ ★ ★

The lump is removed and my Deb is back home
I lay with her daily just us two alone
We lay here and cuddle each other so much
We're quickly becoming the other ones crutch

The kids are fantastic they each do their bit
They help with the chores and with their Mum sit
They're wonderful people so good and so fine
I'm proud every day to know they are mine

The month is now August the day twenty fifth
We go back tomorrow with upper lip stiff
The results they will tell us there's nowhere to hide
Please God be good news for my beautiful bride

To be continued…

Contentment

Dennis Shrubshall

If the simple life is the one you choose
You've lots to gain and little to lose
For monetary gain doesn't measure wealth
It's sometime's measured in happiness and health
And with these two assets ,you'll little need
Ill gotten gains of those with greed
Who by devious actions will only succeed
To bring about their own demise
When the healthy and happy can capitalise
And live in a world of contentment

Let History Not Repeat Itself

Ajibike Lapite

The future promises of many things – almost everything
but none of that means a thing
not when our future is stuck in the past
a future stuck in a past tormented by war

How can we existed while blood escapes, from our soldier's faces?
while death tolls raise at an astounding pace
while innocents pay the price
innocents paying the price for the idiocracy of war

where is the peace that desire us, even at the pyres
by cruel hands dousing peace in a fire
will the world ever learn?
the world learning not to turn to war?

peace is its own reward – a solution of discord
peace solves problems without ever pulling a sword
and God if peace could come here
if peace could save us from what we should avoid – war

Beach

Andrew Papworth

The dark and swirling black cloud fills the sky with its noxious fumes,
Its caustic form stings eyes and darkens minds,
We arrived in expectance,
Hoping that our stand would weather the onslaught,
Yet we leave defeated,
And seem unable to find our place in this new world.

My chest is touching the ground and I look up into fear,
The blackness has swallowed the fading light,
Now, I can only see a spray of hatred,
The bullets of the machine gun flying in a spiral of yellow and orange;
A Catherine Wheel strafing the beach,
A knife slicing through the poisonous air.

A man is cut down next to me,
The bullet removes some of my flesh, and all of his soul,
Behind me are the helmets of our boys,
A human caterpillar stretched into the water like stepping-stones.

A flash of sudden light,
And I will nevermore leave this wretched place.

Behind The Razor Wire

Duncan Prow

A dark and quite moment
When the working day is through
I sit behind the razor wire
My thoughts drift to you

I'm a fit and able soldier
In a war that should not be
Whilst brother you fight a different war
And it lays siege upon your knees

When I here the sirens screaming
Mortars coming in!
I can run and dive for cover
Until it's safe to move again

For you there are no warning signs
You're already on the floor
Lying until morning
When the pain recedes once more

They teach me, Faith, integrity
They expect courageous deeds
Whilst their colleagues in our government
Deny your basic needs

We are brothers fighting different wars
At home and lands afar
But yours has waged the longer
And been more difficult by far

A dark and quite moment
As the day draws to its end
We sit behind the razor wire
Soldiers, Brothers, Friends

Grumpy Old Man

David Killelay

Grumpy Old Man, no such thing
He gave you his Love and a wedding ring

Grumpy Old Man, he was like a Lad
He was the one that you called Dad

Grumpy Old Man, whose life you Share
He's like that because of Love and Care

Grumpy Old Man, as he reads the news
He's so appalled at these modern views

Grumpy Old Man, he may appear
He's proud of you and loves you dear

Grumpy Old Man in later life
So Lucky really that you're his wife

Forget the stories that you've been told
There May be great satisfaction,
In being Grumpy and Old

For My Warrior Poet

In memory of Maj RAN COOPER

Miche

Short days ago, we lived,
felt dawn, saw sunset glow,
loved and were loved.
Owen said it better than me,
Another Poet, in another place,
that land between the rivers invoked Elliott,
to tell me of his love,
but those were happy times,
when love was born, took root and grew,
in that green and black place of fear.
We were warriors both.
We won our battles, together
but my poet has gone.
His poor pen will scratch no more
in our Kevlar world.
Morning star has gone. It was too good.
People like us aren't meant to be in what they call
the real world

Six Months Later

It's been a while, but with Mac's encouragement I put pen to paper this morning to try and start to describe the nagging beastie that lurks deep within my psyche since my return from Iraq...

BJ Lewis

It feels a lifetime ago since I was there.
But I can still taste the atmosphere, feel the warm air.
We've bid farewell to that war now, we've counted our dead,
We've dusted ourselves down and refocused ahead.

But there's no rest for old soldiers, there's still work to do,
British lives still expire in conflict anew,
As I learn of the bloodshed from the comfort of home
I relive those old feelings and let my thoughts roam.

For although I remember the hardship endured,
There's a voice deep within me that can't be ignored,
It compels my return to the adventure of war,
It wants to feel more alive, like it did do before

The Common Soldier

To all my brothers I never met.

Len Payne

He is called a Common Soldier, he comes from many lands,
He fights in steaming jungles, he dies in desert sands,
He sweats upon the drill square, he fears the sergeants eye,
He is the first to march away, among the first to die.
He cares not for daunting odds, nor seeks a place to hide,
He is but a Common Soldier, with another at his side.

He takes no joy in death or causing hurt to others,
He is but a soldier, and all soldiers are but brothers.
He will though fight his countries foe,
He will pass the point where few men go,
He takes misfortune in his stride,
He takes success with quiet pride.

He is given tawdry medals, to be hung upon his breast,
He is quietly contented, he was called, he passed the test.
He is called a Common Soldier, always fighting in the van,
He is called a Common Soldier, but a very Uncommon Man.

He faced the Roman, Turk and Hun,
He was seen at Vimy and Bull Run,
He served with Monty, Ike and Moore,
He took the heights - he stormed the shore.
He fought his war, for it was the last,
He then fought others, to repeat the past.

He fought again to free Kuwait,
He fought again, but not with hate,
He saw the enemy, a simple man,
He saw the specter of Saadam.

He knew too what must be done,
He knew he might die under desert sun.

He knows his worth for across the lands,
He hears the cheers and marching bands,
He knows too that his time has come,
He knows his duty was bravely done.
He stands alone among the throng,
He is bowed and bent, but inward strong,
He was once a Common Soldier, a small part of the plan,
He was once a Common Soldier, but a very Uncommon Man.

They Call It Victory

Beatrice G Davis

still they come, grief-filled coffins
engulfed by a sea of tears
suppressed rage weighed down by death
how can they rest in peace

others say it is needed, won't back down
continue to plan their tomorrows
ignore lessons from the past
say, this is victory, forget forget

forget until caught up by death
old stories are told and retold
endings colored with condescension, changed
embellished with conceit and haughtiness

young ears hear, respond to the call
don their uniforms
still they come, the grief-filled coffins
in this endless war some call victory

Why Do I Feel So Guilty Because Of The Death Of A Fly?

Chris Green

Last night I watched you struggling
To break through the window glass
And I watched you freezing,
Dying, as all things pass.

Last night I could have moved you inside
To die, perhaps, but warm, at least,
And cared for at your last bedside,
As your life went and you were released.

Last night I rejoiced at your dance
As you failed to find the open window,
Your frenzied need of my warm entrance;
Now you are dead, who shall tell your widow?

Is the life of a fly to be so worthless?
I did not kill you, did I?
Yet I stood by and watched you die, hopeless.
Why do I feel guilty because of the death of a fly?

Advice From An Old Warrior

Based on an article by Gene Ladrier.

Mark Christmas

Spewing into the aisles of the Roxy
to watch 'Groundhog Day' but this
is not the Hollywood version, with its glitz
and glamorous stars, this is my version with
no parallax in time, just the here, the now.

The reel clicks into life, once more my eyes
make me taste the ripening, putrid bodies that
soak up the noon day heat. I sample the copper
flavoured shake on my lips. Taste buds explode
with the sensation of bodily waste fermented with

a tinge of cordite on the sweaty, warm air.
End of the reel, the projectionist refits
a new one but for me its not new,
it's the same one, same ending, if it
ever does? Same terrifyingly, intrusive past.

Each moon rise I raise the shutters, turn the latch
key in hope, to keep the demonic past locked
out. Tonight, however, the sedative will man the
defence barricades, to subdue the advancing hoards
of relentless memories that threaten to over-run.

Tonight, I am prepared to wave
my white flag to them, in a last
unenviable hope the assaults
will cease. Though there is little optimism
left as these adversaries,
take 'NO Prisoners'.

Letters Home

Anne-Marie Spittle

Flower heads sway as the battledress pass,
Lemmings walking to meet their end
Callow youth with ghosts of victories filling their heads
Letters from ancient loves in pockets amass
Like threads of a web to catch memory flies
Pale parchment capturing the spirits of the dead

Love is but a memory of past times
In places of legend made up by the new
The mud had filled the void of remembrance
Now wandering cattle toll the chimes
And minds are sent askew
Buried deep into Saturn's world

Explosions of darkness tear the safe
Sending them scurrying to their holes
To return messages of answer

Oblivion follows and various dancers have the field
Framed by the petals of love
Gatherers begin and patch together lives extinguished
Garlands for mothers at home waiting
But not expecting this bouquet of life lost
And tears ensue
And will not be quenched
As long as war exists in the hearts of the Overlords

Marching Song

A tribute to both my parents

Sally Gardner

My Dad went off to fight the war
Left Mum expecting me.
Home for a hug when I was born,
Then back across the sea.

The beach was full of noise and death
The rear guard was his post
He did his duty on that day
And stayed when all was lost.

From France to Germany they marched
Dunkirk their Waterloo
Thousands of bodies left behind
And Mum thought he'd died, too.

But a boy on a bike brought us wonderful news –
Imprisoned but still alive!
My mother wept with tears of joy
And waited for peace to arrive.

For five long years she told me tales
About my hero Dad,
As she struggled to buy us food and clothes
With the little money we had.

But he didn't come marching back to us.
He was on a stretcher laid;
"You mustn't go near," they said to me
"For him there is no aid."

"Don't touch him! Don't kiss him! You stupid child!
Take her away at once.
Tuberculosis has no cure
You should know that, you dunce."

We followed him round the hospitals
I waited outside the door
I could hear my Mother telling him
About me, as I sat on the floor.

"So bright and pretty, good as gold,"
She never said that to me.
But I saw her cry, which he never did,
And I learned to let things be.
.
.Too young to go to the funeral,
They left me sitting at home.
"Your Dad is gone," they said to me,
"Your Mum is on her own."

"Oh, no, she's not," a silent shout,
"I'm here why can't you see?
I don't need a Dad that I've never had
And all Mum needs is me."

My Mother just won't talk of him
Her eyes they go all wet,
A widow's pension she is given
And free school meals I get.

"Turn off that wireless I just can't bear
The sound of laughter here."
I'm six years old, and the world is bleak
And full of bitter fear.

A heavy silence fills our house,
Though at night I hear Mum cry,

At school I pretend to have a Dad
Till the Headmaster says: "Don't lie!"

No teacher ever tells the class;
'Her dad he died for you'.
He didn't die on the battlefield
So they won't believe it's true.

I work hard and win a scholarship
To a very classy school,
And suddenly everyone's telling my Mum
That she mustn't be such a fool.

"Good heavens, no! On a widow's pay,
What are you thinking of, dear?
We'll all pretend that she didn't pass;
It's out of her league, we fear."

And it nearly worked, Mum, didn't it?
But you thought I'd like to know.
I sometimes think you were proud of me
But you couldn't let it show.

You came from a culture of buttoning up
Of never saying 'I care'
And you worked so hard to keep us both
As there was no dad to share.

I hated you sometimes, soldier Dad
For leaving us on our own
The other kids seemed to have it all
While we battled on alone.

But now I am older than you ever were
And I hope you can feel my pride
In having a Dad who gave his life
So his daughter could survive.

Nice One Harry

The Sandman

Young Harry's quite a chap we've heard he even drinks
cold beers
and he joined the British army with lads he saw as peers
He did a cracking job as well and loved
the whole damned thing
He worked as hard as anyone and (we even hear he sings)

But then he had a problem as he wanted active duty
To serve with all his muckers and then some shooty shooty
Now all were not best pleased with this and some
were quite put off
And people even said that he was nothing but a "toff"

Well, time would tell and what a tale it now has been and said
Young Harry was in the thick of it and he isn't blinkin dead
He worked with all the lads out there, he saved lives every day
By sending baddies presents which sent them on their way

Now like it lots or like it less he proved a thing or two
He showed just what he's made of and served his comrades true
He did a job of courage serving Queen and Country too
A job our boys and girls have done for years for me and you

His tour of duty over he's come back home to say
"I did my bit and proud of it", you can't take that away!
His Dad is rightly proud of him his brother too they tell
(And take my word on this one, his Mums real proud as well)

Now in this little poem writ for Forces Poetry
I salute a proud young member of the Household Cavalry
He served our proud fine nation as so many others do
I say "Well done to Harry" and all the others too.

God bless our Queen and Country and our serving boys and girls
Who daily do their duty where the sounds of war unfurls
To those who gave their lives for us in every war that's been
We thank you every one of you and raise glasses to "The Queen".

Uncle Jack

Destroyer HMS Torrent 22nd-23rd December 1917 Torpedoed by a German submarine off the Maas Lightship.

Rob West

I never knew you, Great Uncle Jack; you went off to war,
But didn't come back.
It was nearly Christmas, in nineteen seventeen,
Of home and family, you and your friends must have dreamed.

In the night you gave your life, making the ultimate sacrifice.
Sunk by a U-boat, in the North sea,
Your eternal resting place, this was to be.

I will think of you this Sunday, and all that you gave,
Along with all the others, from the Crimea to Today,
I will raise a glass, and toast to you all:
"Thank you my heroes, your memories live on"

Uncle Jack

The 11th Hour

Bryn Strudwick

I was shopping in Sainsburys on Sunday when the two minutes silence began,
To remember the dead of a century's wars, that unique invention of man.
I covertly looked around me at the shoppers all silent and still
And the checkout assistant, with head bowed, in front
of her idle till.
And I marvelled at just how quiet it was, where just a few moments before,
The place was alive with the hubbub of sounds, that abound in a crowded store.
And as I studied their faces, some lowered, some staring ahead,
I wondered just what they were thinking in this mark of respect
for the dead.

Some young ones perhaps were impatient, to get on with their shopping again.
It was so long ago when it happened, they hadn't experienced the pain.
But the elderly lady beside me was secretly shedding a tear.
She'd known the horror of war time and suffered the noise
and the fear.
Perhaps she remembered a loved one who went away
not to return.
And, looking around at the world of today, she wondered why
they never learn.

I was too young to know what had happened when the second world war was declared.
Just eighteen months old, a mere toddler. I hadn't yet learned
the word 'scared'.
I didn't notice the shortage of food; I barely remembered
my Dad.

I suppose it's quite true that you really don't miss the things that you've never had.
And the sacrifice Mother had to make to ensure that her family thrived .
I knew nothing about 'til long after; then I marvelled at how she'd survived.
I was eight when it finally ended and Dad arrived home at last
And started to rebuild our lives again and tried to forget what had passed.
As a family we had been lucky, for none of our loved ones were lost.
But I remember the tears in my Mother's eyes when they talked of the terrible cost.

My image of war was fashioned, by films and by books that I read.
I read of our glorious exploits and revelled in enemy dead.
I saw The Dam Busters and cheered with the rest as the water gushed out in full flow.
I didn't think of the thousands who drowned, in the stricken valleys below.
When I played, if it wasn't Red Indians, it was dastardly Germans I shot,
And, like in the films, they died cleanly; it seemed not to hurt them a lot.

In real life of course it's not like that; they don't die without any pain.
As a shell rips a limb off or bullets tear through, they cry out again and again,
And lie in the mud for hours on end with no one to render first aid.
'Til death puts an end to their suffering – and another poppy is made.

The voice on the Tannoy says, "Thank you," and the hubbub
resumes once more.
For life must go on for the living and the tills have to roll
for the store.
We have made our annual gesture and I wonder how much
it's achieved.
I fear, for the planet in general, the message is still not perceived.
For during that two minutes silence, the tide will not
have been turned.
Many more have been killed the world over – and all because
man will not learn.

Picking Petals

Julia Whitehouse

The petals vulnerable and delicate were crushed with water droplets,
They were battered by the wind and the rain, interminably damaged: dead,
Those petals are my son: the wind and water, the war,
The constant deep despair which my mind keeps me in custody since his loss,
The pleading with oneself to be set free from the horrific memory,
The vivid images of murder and deceit that flow through my disturbed mind are horrific,
Things have never been seen like this before, through my own two eyes,
The world so distorted and dark,
I have always known the world to be a happy place; my son's joyous laughter, his youthful singing that danced down my tunnelled ear, confirmed this,
I am a brave woman, so it surprises me slightly when I can no longer continue this charade, his death too much to bear,
Death takes when it is time; guns steal when it is not,
My life now not diluted by love, but a concentrate of pure hatred, repulsion towards the world, is now crippled: I let him go; he never returned,
I did not know, how could I have known, I was not told of the horrors, he always wrote with such enthusiasm,
How could I have known?
No longer shall I only live for my neighbours, smiling when their sons' telegrams reach home,
They will soon fall in front of me, like I did to them, pleading and begging for reassurance that life's cruel game hasn't picked them as its target,
Eventually they get dealt the same fate as mine: their babies dead,

How can I just sit here and let this go on, yet I am a woman, in this society, how can I not,
Everyone has a right to life, and everyone has the right to take theirs, but not others',
I am grossly repulsed, dampened with my tears, but I refuse to just sit here and let this go on,
My son: my petal: my child: my baby: gone,
Her son: her petal: her child: her baby: gone,
Her husband: her petal: her love: her protector: gone: picked,
All consumed by a bullet,
I now know what to do, having questioned this life: its meaning,
I will not sit here and do nothing, I will help,
I will try and make a difference, like my son,
I will fight, fight for the fighting to be over,
I will spread this message: War is not a game which naive young soldiers; boys thought it was at first,
For I wish everyone to hear this; I found out too late,
My son: my life: my petal, was taken,
Taken by a sharp crisp autumn leaf that was lost in a gust,
Taken by the men deluded with power; men who ordered me to let him go.

I Want To Be A Soldier

Nick Taylor

One Minute your in a classroom,
Thumb up bum and mind in neutral.
I want to be a Soldier!
Fight for my country like my Father.

Morning, the Giant spoke to me!
Interested in becoming one of the finest?
That's right being a GUARDSMAN.
What's one of them then?

Sign here go to fields far away,
See what it's like away from home.
Enjoy the open areas and sights,
Take it all in and become one of us.

I don't want to be a WELSH GUARD.
I don't understand the lingo,
Can I be an ENGLISH GUARD?
But still look like you tall and stout.

Short and simple that's how it began,
Took the Silver Shilling, swore the oath.
Caught a train away down to the South,
To be greeted at the gate to the GUARDS DEPOT.

One Year on, twelve months of graft,
I'm tall and stout,
Not an ENGLISH GUARD,
But a proud GRENADIER!

Winter Already Old

Stephen Hill c

Winter already old
Drapes itself in a shroud
Lends itself to the blossom
Its tears of grief are caught
In the budding snowdrop

My Light

Andy

I made a journey years ago
from start to finish I had to go
My map was set my journey long
I knew to do this I must be strong

I started well with guides and friends
But my guides they left their time did end
I carried on with all my mates
And made bad turns I made mistakes

From these I learnt I started new
I found my way my bearing true
But then a war and death it came
It sought out friends by rank and name

It picked them off it took them quick
I couldn't help it made me sick
I saw such things my guides did hide
I wish they were with me by my side

I made it through and then back home
But in the dark I wandered alone
I looked for my torch my shining light
To guide me through my awful plight

I used my torch too much I fear
I used it hard til it leaked tears
I heeded not the voices saying
Your torch is dying light decaying

And as I listened looked and learned
I suddenly realised what I had spurned
All this time I had not seen
how my torch had kept its beam

I thank the lord every day
He let me see my errant way
That in the darkest years of life
My shining torch was my lady wife

Thank you!

The Trench

Andy Cook

Alone I stand nothing to do but stare
At this barren land laid so bare.
Splintered trees lean over squalid trenches
Shadows of their former selves - the proud orchards
That covered this once beautiful rolling land.
Nervous eyes peer over muddy mounds
Listening and waiting – praying – "no more, please, God".
I will go mad all alone – no friends for comfort.

The long dash I will not make
Our lines too far to reach.
I think a German bullet lies in wait
To cross these sodden trenches
And it surely has my name on.
My trench will be my refuge
My safe, lonely place to hide,
Among the rats and my friends the fallen
Down by my side.

The air is still and oh so heavy!
No-one dares to use their eyes
To see such horror on both sides.
Desolate land strewn with dead,
Craters, horses and shattered trees
And now it is so quiet – no sound is made
Am I really all alone? Dare I look?
Trust my God what to do.

Hugging my rifle I stand and stare
Wondering what will be.
The puddles – lakes of tears never drying,
Reflecting the greyness of the day.
The rippling water shows the face of a friend
Who is not really there?
"Have courage," he whispers softly
Giving me the strength to wait for what will be
Life or eternity.

Laughter To Tears

Derek Blackburn

The ginger tom watched from his perch
 On the bombed, broken wall
The children laughed as they
Chased a blue football
Yet in the fields across the dirt track
Beneath the majestic pines
Just waiting to amputate
THE COLD HEARTLESS MINES.

The sun melts the winter snow
In the hills high above
Streams swell into rivulets
Like tears once shed for love
These emerald snakes meander along
Yet amongst this beauty
ONLY DEATH SINGS HIS SONG.

Why do the innocents suffer it all?
From the orphans of carnage
To the kids with their ball
Why can't we stop the need for war?
Please help me to understand
What it's all for.

No More!

(1972–1994)

BZED

No more reveille's, no stand-to,
No waiting in a breakfast queue,
No half fried eggs in pans of oil,
No hot water, hard to boil,
No PT kit to help me run,
No cold sea dips just for some fun,
No racing back to camp at speed, to satisfy some urgent need.
No polishing to make it gleam, no painting grass
to make it green,
or painting coal to make it black, no not much freakin chance
of that.

No reason not to speak my mind and say exactly what I find,
No need to watch just what I say, No interviews without coffee,
No slow march or marking time, no quick march,
nor double time,
No making sure your never late and no more 'hurry up
and wait',
No new COs or RSMs, or fresh from Sandhurst Subalterns,
with fresh ideas to listen to, no not a chance,
I'm freakin through.

No Battle Camps to hone my skills, no digging-in, no Battle
drills,
No forced marches all gung-ho, to fight a non-existent foe,
No passwords, recce's or 'O' Groups, no consorting with
the troops,
No soggy maggot for a bed or bivvy slung above my head,
No cries of 'End Ex' or 'Stand Down', no pack up kit and
hit the town,
Into the nearest bar we find… to right the wrongs of all mankind.

No more recruits to educate, no more trained soldiers to update,
No more courses EPC, First-Aid, Weapons, NBC.
AMI or CFT and no more freakin BFT's
No more range days in the rain, and running back
to Camp again,
some circuit training 'for a change'… I'd rather run back
to the range.
Inspections every other day… thank Christ… for me…
they've gone away.

No Reggie dinners in the Mess, best bib and tucker to impress,
No five course meal with Sunday roast, no 'Pass the Port' with
'Loyal Toast'
The waiting Staff receive our thanks, then onwards with our
foolish pranks,
No drinking long into the night, and walking? Home in broad
daylight.
High spirits mixed with alcohol, ensured our members had
a Ball,
Alas, too much for one or two,
and 'Extras' went where 'Extras' due.

No MFO and no A10's, Should never have to move again
With no March out and no March in, at last a house to settle in.
So no more soldiering for me, no uniforms or cards ID,
No 'GRIT' with 'CLAP' no more TP's, just civvy street
and memories.
No need for bullshit every day, a fair days work for fair days pay,
that's how it works here, so they say, so 'Carpe Diem'
or 'seize the Day'.

I've 'Carpe Diemed' for fifteen years and kept my distance
from my peers,
ashamed they thought I missed my Corps or better yet, I missed
them more,
No honestly!, that's not the case, I've just been busy in this place,
Trying just to be like them, a hard working, honest, citizen.

but recently it has dawned on me, that all those years of military,
Were not as bad as they might be, much better than
those presently.

For people such as you and I… ex RD and MTI's,
We thrived on challenges each day, "What's that?, not me!",
I hear you say,
You lying twat, you loved it too, It's what we lived for,
me and you,
Not content, like all the rest, we all aspired to be the best,
We gave our all and then some more, for our beloved,
Ordnance Corps,
Alas now gone, just like our trade, forgotten,
as our memories fade.

We muster now within this Board, recanting tales
of long past wars,
Of characters within our Corps and stories from our many tours,
Remembering mates now passed and gone, united now
on this Forum
Old friends absent from Parade, not a problem, new ones made,
Time to form up, what a sight! Dead on the Left,
Us on the Right,
The new guard bring up the rear, what now for those
assembled here?
Who, not content just marking time, The 'Gathering, two
thousand nine'.

"SPARTANS! This year we dine in…

Somebody Somewhere

Alison Mitchell

Oh where do those big blue beautiful eyes go, when you're not
at one with me,
Perhaps to your world of contentment where everything's safe
and sound,
I wish for you to be in my world if only for just one day,
It wasn't to be, and what you've achieved has made me
so terribly proud.
Your love of tractors trains and trucks, is like every little boys.
You line them up with so much skill, they call it obsessive
behavior,
I see it differently to them I see a little boy deep in play,
with dedication an passion, It's these words I choose to favour.
Each day a new that unravels with wondrous things to learn,
you look, you listen without any comment, but store
for future date.
I ask what shall we do today? You say can I have a biscuit
this weekend,
I know what you mean, but they call it inappropriate.
That was when you were five, and now you have got to eight,
We fought the LEA and now hope the path is becoming straight,
Life is always going to be an uphill struggle I know that is for sure
But the pleasure you bring into ours life's out ways its
ten times more
You still like the daily routine, and keep things in
the same old place
You still hate twisty socks and bendy pants! every morning
we still have to face
We both have lots of learning, to understand each others lives
and woes,

I promised I will try to keep finding socks, which won't annoy your toes.
You make me so happy with your funny quirky ways, your odd little dances, off into your dances you go son,
The love I feel is too much to put into words, what ever our future, we'll fight it together your ever loving mum.

Dear Mr Read

David Bean

I'm sorry, I didn't mean to see.
I should explain – we haven't met,
I've only seen you once as yet.
I went upstairs just after tea
and saw you then. Did you see me?
Is that the best suit you could get?
It must feel good, I bet,
to be free.

Last year in the Mall we celebrated,
saw VE flags file through the arch.
But you weren't there – we should have waited –
you were still in Burma, not on the march.
This evening you were sat on the lawn, alone.
Was I very wrong to look?
I'd only gone to fetch a book.
Why are you skin and bone?

The skeleton of memory
stuck out as I watched
when VJ soldiers marched
the Mall belatedly.
Stuttering, shuffling steps they took
with looks of pride, limbs that groaned,
emaciated, moaned,
haunted by guardian gook.

I've taken sixty years to see.
A thousand VJ stars parade
without you, Mr. Read,
celebrate you posthumously,
saluted now by royalty.
My full-sobbed tears do not degrade.
We meet at last, with pride.

Brief Encounter

Jenny Martin

Your Daddy's off to his training,
there's a war on, you must not cry,
they said when he left on a troop train.
Training-war-train-do-not-cry
baffled my three-year-old mind.

Three years with a few brief encounters
when he returned home on leave
shrouded in battledress khaki
apart from his boots. They were black
like Lancaster's soot-soiled stone-work,
sky split by searchlights at night,
sleep nightmared by air-raids and sirens.
Morecambe Bay's radiant sunsets
greyed-out in my mind.

On our brief encounter before D-Day
at my aunt's home near calm Windermere Lake
evening's candle- and lamp-light
glowed warm in my mind.

We left Windermere station together
but my father would stay on the train
on his way to a Normandy beach.
At Lancaster we would leave him: life's colours
greyed-out in my mind.

Before then the train stopped at Carnforth
where tea-ladies sought out the soldiers.
With a smile one handed my father
a jam-jar of golden-brown tea.
Good luck, safe return, she wished him: dead colours
revived in my mind.

Carnforth tea-ladies long departed.
Who cares today for our soldiers?
Or their families' once living colours
greyed-out in their minds?

Snapshots Of War

Rachael Willis

Dice tumble from the tower of reason,
shattering lives and illusions
with indiscriminate ease;
men, women, friends and lovers
forced to play a fateful game
of impossible, inevitable odds.

Acts of uncompromising heroism,
born out of necessity and discipline,
driven by a will greater than our own,
fire men from the safety of their kin,
elevating them above the humanity
they profess to represent.

News filters into our consciousness
like sand into sights –
obscuring in its overwhelming clarity –
while rhetoric, applauded and derided,
seeps through the cracks
of the bloodied ledger.

The indelible stamp of history,
Justifying, celebrating, betraying
This generation to the next.

He Said

Written about my grandad

Anwen Hayward

He said that the moon was pale,
A silver sliver in the choking night,
And that it illuminated their prison like cobwebs in a candle.
The deafening thuds and crashes filled
The dusty, dangerous air,
And lived in harmony with the drowning gases.
The ground was thick and uninhabitable,
So even the simple weeds had withered,
But his pride and sense of duty remained intact.
He said that men were lost each time he blinked,
So he did not close his eyes for fear of missing his friend,
Or a bullet.
Those who died were left behind,
In panic rather than disgrace,
And where they lay, a dusting of vermillion grew
That hid the smears of crimson caked into the earth,
Running into puddles of filth,
Contaminating where he was forced to cower.
He said that even the Sun could not shine a light
On the reasons for their destruction,
Because it was hiding from the enemy.
The stars shrank, wilted,
Like the hope of the men he called his brothers,
And when they died, the stars passed too.
The atmosphere was thick and smoky
With the remnants of gunfire
And the despair of the men.

He said that one evening, all was still
Yet his eyes were open, taking in reality
And he could hear the others breathe
As everyone that crouched in the trenches and the shell holes
Put down their weapons
And cried a new colour.

Info

Alexandrine

There is no mystery
in the information age.
just knowledge of the unwanted
on every pristine web page.
everything you want is at your fingertips
except her lips.
except your heart's desire.
except her breath beside you,

you're in love's eclipse.

you're in hells abyss,
and you wish she'd have the balls to miss you
the feet to run and kiss you
the eyes to see your glowing soul,
which matches hers so blissful.

i go to sleep thinking of the lonely lyric
that there is no info on my spirit.

Too Many Times

Charles Savage

I know that your talking
Telling tales full of pride
But your eyes tell a story
That your smile fails to hide
And I know that your hurting
Cause I'm not there by your side
I've said goodbye too many times

I know its not easy
On your own with the boys
Trying to be happy
As you play with their toys
But you know when I left
That I had no choice
I've left you alone too many times

But, when I return,
There'll be a smile just for me
And a sparkle in your eyes,
Cause we're a four instead of three
And you worked hard through it all
To hold together our family
So I can't say I love you too many times

I love you

Blue

Robert Jenkins

A mid-winter morning;
The sky a uniform grey:
Everything sodden; Puddles aplenty;
Me, up to my eyes in debt and struggling;
My youngest daughter in hospital,
Recovering from an overdose;
But it's cool, not cold,
And the rain has stopped.
One or two birds are singing.
Green Daffodil spears pierce the leaf mould.
On a nearby branch, a dove woos his lover.
My debt management plan is all but in place.
My little girl is loved. She will be okay.
That other little girl, my Grand-daughter,
Considers my question;
"What colour is the sky?"
Her eyes flick to a tiny rent overhead
And she replies unhesitatingly,
"Blue!"
I think so too.

If you have enjoyed this book, you may interested in similar titles from SilverWood Books.

All our titles are available to order from bookshops, or online at www.silverwoodbooks.co.uk.

Voices of the Poppies – An Anthology of Poetry
(Introduced by Dame Vera Lynn DBE)
ISBN 9781906236076
£8.99
(Proceeds to FLOW for All)

Stories of the Poppies – A Short Story Collection Volume 1
ISBN 9781906236267
£8.99
(Proceeds to FLOW for All)

A Tapestry of Verse
by Dennis Shrubshall
ISBN 9781906236144
£8.99
(proceeds shared between The British Limbless ex Servicemen's Association, Combat Stress, and The National Gulf Veterans and Families Association)

Overpaid, Over-Sexed and Over There
(The Adventures of a Limey in the US Army)
by Chris Holloway
ISBN 9781906236168
£8.99

Surviving Changi – A Memoir
(With illustrations by kind courtesy of Ronald Searle)
by Peter Gordon Kendall
ISBN 9781906236014
£14.00